H

by

"Spectator"

Published by

RACEFORM LTD.

Compton, Newbury, Berkshire RG16 0NL

HOW TO WIN AT RACING by Spectator

First published 1962
Second impression 1967
Third impression 1971
Fourth impression 1982
Fifth impression 1987
Sixth impression 1992

ISBN 0 900611 67 7

Published by Raceform Ltd.,
Compton, Newbury, Berkshire RG16 0NL
Printed by Bocardo Press Ltd., Didcot.

CONTENTS

HOW TO WIN AT RACING

Since the last edition of this book was published, the on-course betting tax has been lifted, although there is still heavy duty on off-course bets. Having added the Levy, most off-course bookmakers round-up their deductions to 10%. It is therefore most important that the backer should go racing as often as possible and bet without tax. That way he really has got a chance to win at racing. Also, remember that if you are thinking of having a substantial ante post bet, do not grab the telephone or go to your local betting shop, but set off for the nearest racemeeting and have your bet there.

There are many ways of having a bet. You can spin a coin, turn a card or bet on the outcome of football matches. But in my opinion racing gives its followers much the most interest, win or lose. The sport is extremely well covered in this country by press and television. In addition, there is a wide range of specialist publications which enable the backer to become very knowledgeable.

The purpose of this book is to introduce new avenues to the racing enthusiast whose interest to date may have been somewhat superficial.

SPECTATOR

Raceform Ltd.
Compton,
Newbury,
Berkshire RG16 0NL
February 1992

I. THE IMPORTANCE OF FORM

THE title "How to Win at Racing" at once begs the question, is it possible to make money backing horses?

The vast majority of punters obviously are losers. If this were not the case there would not be so many long-term survivors among the bookmakers and indeed survivors who clearly prosper.

When the last edition of this book was published, there was a 4% betting tax on-course. Even this amount had effectively wiped out the professional racecourse backers, who expected to make 2½% profit on turnover in an average year and perhaps 5% in a good one.

The astute backer once again has a chance of turning a long-term profit on-course but to do so with a 10% tax off-course is clearly going to be very hard indeed. The moral of this is to go racing on every possible occasion and to bet sparingly away from the course thereby increasing the proportion of winners compared with losers. The sensible backer intent on a sizeable ante-post bet will visit the racecourse in order to place it, thus saving himself 10%.

The present Aga Khan's grandfather, one of the shrewdest men ever to go racing, was once asked whether the average backer could expect to make money backing horses.

He replied: "If the punter takes the trouble, he certainly will win . . . he must work very hard, look it up, follow form, follow form, follow public form."

Fortunately, the study of form provides endless interest and amusement. There is great satisfaction in reaching your own conclusions about a race and knowing exactly why you are going to back a particular horse.

FORM = FACT + OPINION; but for form to be of any value, the facts must be completely accurate and the opinions must be of an expert nature.

However, even the most enthusiastic racegoer cannot be everywhere at once and so everyone must rely to a considerable extent upon other people's reports. These are available in *Raceform* (The Jockey Club's Official Form Book), *Raceform Update* and *Raceform Note-Book*, on behalf of which skilled race-readers and paddock critics attend every race meeting.

In form, fact ends and opinion takes over at an early stage. That three-year-old colt Alpha ridden by Smith beat three-year-old colt Beta ridden by Jones, over 10 furlongs at Epsom on June 4th, each carrying 9 st. is a fact. But the distance of three lengths between them at the finish is an opinion, albeit officially expressed by the judge.

That Alpha started at odds of 3/1 and Beta at 4/1 is the opinion of the representatives of The Press Association and *The Sporting Life*, who are responsible for making the Starting Price returns. Such items of opinion are unlikely to be disputed and the foregoing will be the basis of the official result of the race as recorded by Messrs. Weatherby who are Secretaries to the Jockey Club, racing's governing body.

Racehorses tend to run remarkably true to form and if Alpha and Beta were to meet again under similar conditions it is very likely that Alpha would again finish ahead of Beta.

However, weight is a great leveller and a different result could be obtained by adjusting the amount of weight carried by each.

The effect of weight can be directly equated to distance and the following table is generally acceptable to students of form:

Length of course	Difference produced at finish		
	Half length	Three quarters	One length
5f	1 lb.	2 lb.	3 lb.
6f—10f	1 lb.	1 lb.	2 lb.
11f and over	—	1 lb.	1 lb.

Thus, strictly on their form at Epsom, Alpha and Beta could be expected to run a dead heat if Alpha were given 6 lb. more to carry than Beta.

Now let us suppose, for example, that they meet again in August at York over 12 furlongs and that Alpha is set to carry 9st. 6lb. and Beta 9st. Before taking a view about this encounter, we should want to delve more deeply than the bare bones of the Epsom result.

Here follow some of the other factors which can have a

bearing on the York race. They are dealt with under nine headings: Breeding, Jockeyship, The Paddock, The Market, The Running, Time, The Draw, Going and The Course.

Before proceeding, we must revert for a moment to the table above showing the effect of weight on distance at the finish. Most official and unofficial handicappers are inclined to scale down the weight allowance in the case of horses finishing more than four lengths behind the winner. It is impossible to lay down any hard and fast rules about this as discretion obviously must be used. When the distances become extended, one must try and assess not only how much the winner had up his sleeve at the finish but also to what extent his pursuers may have been eased when their task became hopeless. These points are discussed more fully in section 5, headed The Running.

So far as Jumping is concerned, the normal allowance is 1lb. for a length in two mile hurdles and ½ lb. for a length in two and a half and three mile hurdle races. For steeplechasers, 1 lb. is a reasonable allowance up to two and a half miles, and ½ lb. for races in excess of that distance. When the going is very testing, many experts are inclined to halve these weight allowances.

1. *Breeding*

THE distance of Alpha and Beta's race at York is two furlongs further than at Epsom. If neither horse has attempted the longer distance, breeding may give the best clue to his ability to get the trip.

If Alpha's sire and dam respectively never won over more than a mile, it is not likely that Alpha will be at his best over one and a half miles. On the other hand, if Beta's parents were both out-and-out stayers, Beta reasonably can be expected to be better at twelve furlongs than at ten.

Anyone who has been following racing for several years will automatically acquire some knowledge of breeding, as he will remember many of the sires and some of the dams as racehorses. The Form Book also gives the sire of the dam, which provides some clue to the latter if she is an unknown name. Life has been made more difficult by the influx of American-breds in recent years involving a vast array of sometimes little-known stallions.

Even if he did not know the sire on the racecourse, there is an invaluable guide to the stamina of his progeny produced at the end of each season by *The Statistical Record*. This list, which is reproduced in the front of *Raceform Note-Book*, shows the average distance in furlongs of races won to-date at three years and upwards by every sire's progeny. The list produced at the end of 1990, for example, showed that Absalom's offspring won at an average of 7.0 furlongs, while Warpath's averaged 12.7. Then there may be full brothers with exactly the same parentage and half brothers with the same dam whose racing career will be a further guide.

Each stallion may service forty or more mares a year and thus many more mares are used for breeding than stallions. There are in fact hundreds of mares at stud whose racecourse careers have been brief, undistinguished and sometimes nonexistent. It is often considered adequate for a nicely bred filly to win one small race before being hurried off to the paddocks.

Apart from stamina, other characteristics may be transmitted from parents to their progeny. For instance, some families may be quiet and lazy in temperament, while others may be excitable and nervous. Then again, a sire, who is bad in the wind or has unsound legs, may produce offspring similarly afflicted. Thus a sound, well tested handicapper can prove a better proposition as a stallion than an unsound, lightly raced classic winner.

Some stallions habitually get precocious winning two-year-olds who may fail to train on, while others produce late maturing stock who seldom win before their second season. The idea, which is advocated in certain quarters, that some stallions' progeny of a certain colour are soft, cannot be scientifically supported any more than can the old wive's tale about four white socks.

The breeding of jumpers is of minor significance. Apart from those got by a handful of leading sires of steeplechasers, most jumpers nowadays were originally bred for flat racing.

2. *Jockeyship*

NEEDLESS to say the man on top is a vitally important consideration. In fact, many shrewd racegoers go so far as to confine their bets strictly to horses ridden by top flight jockeys and maybe they save themselves money by so doing.

Some horses will go perfectly well for an apprentice, but others need strong handling by an experienced rider. A stuffy, lazy horse will need a powerful jockey to drive him hard if he is to show his best. Then there is the type of animal who must not hit the front too soon and has to be brought with a very late run to win his races right on the post. Such horses naturally require expert handling.

American and Australian jockeys are supreme as judges of pace. They have been used to doing home gallops with the stop watch timing every furlong. The best of them are brilliant at delivering their challenge right on the line and an unreliable horse or a green two-year-old will scarcely realise he has had a race. French-based jockeys, who are used to a slow early pace, can find themselves in deep water when they come to England and find a fast run race is all over before they can deliver their devastating final sprint.

The weight allowance can obviously give the best apprentices the edge over fully fledged jockeys, provided the horse concerned is the type of animal who will run kindly for them. The apprentice sometimes has to do no more than sit still. If he succeeds in riding his mount to best advantage, the weight allowance must prove a decisive race winning factor.

With the run of the mill apprentice, on the other hand, inexperience generally more than offsets the allowance and the boy will not be a particularly good proposition to beat his seniors. In other words, it is usually better to have a competent and fully fledged jockey than a boy with an allowance.

Apprentices seem to be at less of a disadvantage in handicaps than in weight for age races, probably because handicaps tend to be run at a truer pace and thus riding tactics play a less important part.

Most big stables retain a competent jockey so that they can always be sure of having a first class pilot at their disposal. They also find it advantageous to have a good man available to ride work at home, to get to know the horses before partnering them on the racecourse and to report on progress in the race itself.

It is often significant when a small stable books a top jockey on whom it has no retainer, especially if he is riding close to his minimum weight. Invariably the horse concerned is either strongly fancied to win, or the partnership is being prepared for success in some future event.

Follow the man in form is a particularly apt adage when it comes to jockeys. So often everything seems to go right with those who are enjoying a successful run. A string of winners gives most jockeys added confidence; and attempts at difficult tactics and daring manoeuvres have a habit of coming off for those riding on the crest of the wave. Moreover, the men in form get the best mounts, as owners and trainers tend to overlook jockeys who are not currently riding winners. Those who are out of luck seem to stay out of luck, losing dash and confidence and failing on horses on which they should have won.

Most backers shun races confined to apprentices, but it is a fact that they have a habit of working out true to form. *Raceform Private Handicap*, for example, has a good record at showing apprentice race winners best-in, often at long odds. The reason for this must be that the horses run their own race with the minimum influence from the saddle. Before making an investment, however, it is as well to know that the apprentice concerned has some competence.

Amateur races on the flat are best left alone, although the top riders can be worth several pounds and it can pay to follow them without worrying too much about the relative form of the horses.

A brand of amateur event which is often a good medium for speculation is the Hunter 'Chase. These races are run from the beginning of February until the end of the jumping season. The competitors, both equine and human, traverse a wide range of quality, the best being very good and reliable, while many of the others are . . . well, just hunters. The best of them are well worth following and their odds often represent excellent value, even if they are short, as so often there is very little to beat.

3. *The Paddock*

THE backer who is fortunate enough to be able to go racing will find it worthwhile to inspect the horses in the parade ring before each event, especially the two-year-olds. Considerable experience and a certain amount of natural ability is required to get maximum profit from these observations. The best way is to find someone who is prepared to give some tuition in the subject. After a while you will be able to judge for yourself which are the good lookers, which are really muscled-up and fit, which are backward etc.

Some useful paddock pointers, however, can be gained by the complete novice. A sweating horse, for example, is probably nervous especially if the day is cool. He is expending valuable energy which could be better employed in the race itself. A horse with bandaged ankles may have become sore through galloping on hard ground.

A horse at his best generally will look bright in his coat and in his demeanour. He will be well muscled-up, with nice round quarters and a good firm line to his neck. Tell-tale signs of unfitness are a pot belly and slackness over the loins.

Beware also of animals behaving badly, or coltishly, as their minds are not on racing, or neighing to a marked extent as this usually indicates greenness.

Paddock observations published after the running of the race can be most useful when making calculations about future events. For example *Raceform's* comment that a horse has done well from a physical point of view is very often followed by an improved performance and possibly a win. Again, so far as sweating is concerned, it may be seen from the Form Book that a particular horse always sweats before his races and that he is quite capable of winning nonetheless.

The majority of two-year-olds are described in *Raceform* the first time they run in public. One who merits "v nice c" (very nice colt) can be expected to reach the top flight, while "useful" implies that the animal should be capable of finding a race sooner or later.

Returning to our tale of Alpha and Beta, we may find that Beta's Epsom race was his first outing of the season and that the *Raceform* paddock critic noted that he was backward. It is thus reasonable to suppose that the race will have brought him on and that he should put up a relatively better performance against Alpha at York two months later.

Blinkers have often been referred to as the rogue's badge, but this is not necessarily so. There are many horses as honest as the day is long, who just seem to go better in blinkers. On the other hand, it is not generally a very good sign when a two-year-old makes his racecourse debut wearing this equipment.

It is quite usual for a horse to show a marked improvement in form the first time he wears blinkers, but on subsequent appearances blinkers may not necessarily have such a beneficial effect.

Retired *Raceform* paddock critic Miss Diana Matthews, recently wrote: "Whether one can pick winners purely by paddock inspection is a highly debatable point, but it is, on the other hand, fair to say that the person who backs a horse for other reasons without looking at him first is betting with incomplete knowledge."

4. *The Market*

MONEY talks and never so eloquently as in racing. It naturally adds substantial weight to any argument about a horses's prospects if connections are prepared to support their fancy with hard cash.

The betting market before a race can provide many pointers and it is most instructive to watch the price fluctuations whether you are at the races, in a betting shop, or in front of a television set.

The bookmakers only set the opening prices, which will be based on past form and their own excellent information service. From then on the price changes are dictated by demand and supply. A runner well backed by connections or other knowledgeable people will contract in price, whereas one that is ignored in the market will be offered at a longer and longer price as bookmakers attempt to attract money for him.

In the Epsom race in which Alpha and Beta were involved, Beta may have opened as favourite at 2/1, on the strength of his form the previous season. Alpha, on the other hand, may have opened at 5/1. Knowing that Beta is not at peak fitness, the stable may refrain from betting. As a result, Beta "drifts" in the market. This "drift" tends to be accentuated by the strong support for Alpha, who is expected to show improved form by his owner and trainer. Eventually Alpha starts at 3/1 and Beta at 4/1. All this will be recorded briefly in *Raceform Note-Book* after the running comments. (3/1: op 5/1) will appear after Alpha's and (4/1: op 2/1) after Beta's. This information will be most useful when assessing the York race. The horse which has been well backed is more likely to have run up to his best form, whereas the horse which has faded in the market may be capable of something better in the future.

The betting, though, can be deceptive on occasions. Some stables do not bet and their charges are likely to go out in price, however well fancied, in face of strong support for other runners. Then again, at important meetings like Royal Ascot and the Cheltenham Festival there is such a volume of money in circulation and the market is so strong, that quite a sizeable bet from an owner or trainer can pass almost unnoticed. Unfortunately, nowadays, the betting market has become pathetically weak at many run-of-the-mill meetings. As a result, a little money can cause quite violent price fluctuations and these are sometimes deliberately engineered by off-course bookmakers who may have big liabilities over accumulator bets.

But by and large the betting market is a fine guide which should be closely observed.

Unless you have inside information about a longshot, it does not usually pay to rush in and take opening prices. You will notice from the betting boards in the shops and also on television that most prices drift and only a few tighten up. This is because bookmakers tread warily with their opening prices. It is said that the best time to strike a bet is just before the off. If you cannot manage that it is best to content yourself with starting price.

5. *The Running*

RACECOURSE performance provides the best pointer to future prospects.

Even the television viewer will see plenty that is of interest for the future. In fact, from the remote cameras, incidents often can be observed which are not visible to racegoers in the stands.

Television race viewing, however, is limited by narrow vision. The viewer has to rely on the commentator and the camera operator, and his interest is confined largely to what they choose to point out.

Jumping is often particularly unsatisfactory on television when fields become strung out and the camera can only take in a few of the runners.

The only completely satisfactory way of reading a race is from a good position as high in the stands as possible and through a first class pair of binoculars with a wide field of vision.

Before the runners enter the Parade Ring, check over the owners' colours as published in the racecard, and make a note of any colour changes which may appear on the number board. When the jockeys enter the Paddock, take a close look at any silks or jerseys which are not familiar. You will find many of them are not quite what you imagined from the racecard description, especially if colours have become faded.

Get to your chosen vantage point on the grandstand in good time and wait for the runners to pass on their way to the post. As they come by, test yourself on the colours and firmly fix those in your mind which are new to you. Obviously, the more you go racing the more colours will become familiar and the less preliminary work will be necessary.

As they go to post, watch each horse's action. Some may be striding out well on the going, while others may move unimpressively and thus show that they do not appreciate the underfoot conditions.

A word of warning, though. Sometimes a horse who moves unimpressively to the start at half speed will confound his detractors by coming home faster than anything else.

When the last runner is on his way, you may wish to have a bet. Do this as quickly as possible and return to your place in the stand. You will have had scarcely any time to observe market movements but you may have been able to jot down opening prices before you went to the Paddock. You thus will at least be able to note major fluctuations. Don't forget, patience is a virtue and there is no need to force yourself to have a bet in every race. To avoid a loser is as good as being on an even money winner.

Once back on the stands, focus your glasses on the start. The draw, which is marked on the racecard will help you to identify the colours before they go into the starting stalls and come "under starter's orders". The runners always line up from the left, so if you are facing towards them, the horse drawn number one will be to your right. Many of the silks will look rather different at a distance, as only the predominant colours on body and cap will show up.

Keep your eyes on the start and be ready for the "off". There they go! Watch for the slow starters and for those who are not too quickly into their stride. Then range your glasses forward to the front of the field to see which horses are making the early pace.

Try to ignore the public commentator. By reading the race yourself you will see much more. If you find that you cannot remember a certain set of colours, do not start searching through your racecard. Just try to memorize them and identify them after the race.

As the field settles down range your eyes backwards and forwards, identifying the runners. As they get to about halfway, it is interesting to note which ones are apparently pressed to hold their place and which seem full of running. Maybe one or two jockeys already will be showing signs of uneasiness. On a straight course with the runners coming towards you, it may be difficult to tell which side of the field is in the lead. A path across the course or landmarks on opposite sides of the course can give you the answer.

There will be a great temptation to keep your eyes riveted on any horse you have backed. But this urge must be sternly resisted if you are to get maximum value from watching the race so far as the future is concerned.

It is the last few furlongs of running which will prove most instructive. Here the non-stayers will drop back while horses who could not go the early pace may make up a deal of ground, thus showing that they might prefer a shorter or longer distance respectively. Only with experience will you learn to judge whether a horse's stamina is giving out at the finish or whether he lacks speed to go with the leaders and in fact would be suited by a longer distance. Deceptively, a horse who is staying on at one pace at the finish while all the others are stopping may appear to inexperienced eyes to be producing a blinding burst of speed.

You may spot a jockey who is unable to bring his mount through into a challenging position. He may find himself boxed in on the rails or stuck behind a wall of horses. By the time he gets through, the race may be over. Note this one for another time, although it generally does not pay to take too much notice of hard luck stories which were not confirmed by your own eyes.

Also, you may note a horse or two whose jockeys appear incapable of getting the best out of them. These may be worth backing on some future occasion when they have the benefit of a top line pilot.

When the whips really begin to crack and the final battle is joined, it is interesting to see which horses run on straight and true and which appear to lack heart for the struggle.

At the winning post, your own observations may tell you a good deal more than do the official distances. For example, Alpha's three lengths win over Beta at Epsom may have been gained with such ease as to have left the impression that Alpha could have made the margin six lengths had his rider so desired. On the other hand, Alpha may have been ridden flat out, while Beta was eating up ground at the finish and was still full of running as he reached the post. For future reference, the running comments in *Raceform* and *Raceform*

Update will be expressed thus:

Alpha . . . *v. easily* . . . or alternatively, *strongly ridden*
Beta . . . *late headway, ran on strongly*

Do not keep your eyes glued on the placed horses. As the winner passes the post, it is instructive to look back and spot runners who, but for being eased, might have finished much closer.

Even when the race is all over, it may yet yield further information to the enterprising spectator. Try to get along to the winner's enclosure and to the outlying parts of the Paddock where the "also rans" are being led in. This excursion may reveal animals who are blowing hard and will clearly benefit from the good gallop they have just had, and others which are hard trained and "could not blow out a candle". Such observations may confirm or deny pre-race impressions gained from the Parade Ring inspection.

Likewise, it is almost always rewarding to watch a replay of the running on closed circuit television or on the video at home.

It is doubtful whether one racegoer in a hundred will go to the trouble of reading a race in the manner outlined above. The vast majority will do little more than keep their eyes on the runner they have backed. But the exceptional racegoer will find that his observations will yield him a rich harvest in the future.

To read a race so that it is of real value for the future requires plenty of practice and a certain amount of natural talent. The majority of racegoers probably never acquire the art to any advanced degree, and in any case cannot attend every meeting. It is thus necessary to depend to a greater or lesser extent upon *Raceform, Raceform Update* and/or *Raceform Note-Book*, which report on the running of every race at every meeting.

At all meetings, *Raceform's* race-reads are compiled by two or even three observers. Their comments can usefully be supplemented by the subscriber's own observations from those meetings which he is able to attend.

6. *Time*

In such places as the U.S.A. and Australia, with their dependable weather, centralised racing and standardised tracks, the stop-watch and the sectional timing play an important part in racing. In this country, however, the changeable weather and vast variety of courses makes Time a somewhat undependable factor. Nevertheless, the clock has a useful role to play in telling us whether a race has been run at a true pace and, therefore, whether the form is likely to be reliable. It is also useful in comparing the respective ability of horses when no form line exists between them, particularly two-year-olds in the early weeks of the season.

First and foremost, though, it is essential that accurate time recordings should be available. there is no difficulty at the following tracks, which employ electric timing apparatus and publish an official time for every race: Ascot, Ayr, Chester, Doncaster, Epsom, Goodwood, Haydock, Kempton, Lingfield, Newbury, Newcastle, Newmarket, Salisbury, Sandown and York. However, unofficial hand timing is still the order of the day at the remaining courses, which is ridiculous as the time of a horse race should be regarded just as much as part and parcel of the result as it is at an athletics meeting. It is a sad comment on racecourse executives that none has installed electric timing since the early sixties when those listed above did so with the aid of the Levy Board.

It has been found that, on average, a human being will return a time which is half a second faster than the machine on account of the interval it takes for light to travel, the brain to react and the thumb to operate. But this lapse of time is in itself unimportant provided it is constant.

To produce a consistent and reliable set of times, the watch-holder must keep his eyes riveted on the starting stalls, waiting for the gates to open, and he must be positioned as close to the winning line as possible so that he can judge the precise moment at which the winner passes the post. For some races where the start is out of sight, the watch-holder has to rely on the fall of the white flag. This introduces a big element of unreliability.

The times returned by *Raceform* are generally regarded as highly accurate. Alongside each, both *Raceform* and *Raceform Note-Book* print its variation from Raceform Standard Time for course and distance. These standard times, which are all-important for any further calculations, have been computed from times taken over a period of years on good going. Extremes of going have been ignored as they produce freak times. Standard Time is an average of the ten best times over the course and distance adjusted to 9 stone.

A time which is substantially slower than Standard

suggests that the early part of the race has been run at an unusually slow pace and that the race itself is thus suspect as a guide to future form.

Conversely a race run close to Standard Time or better than Standard Time is more likely to be a completely reliable guide to the future.

If the time for the Epsom race between Alpha and Beta were five seconds slower than Standard in spite of the going being described as firm, we can assume that the slow pace helped Alpha to overcome his non-staying pedigree and to get the distance. Beta, who is bred to stay, would not on the other hand have been suited by the slow pace.

Record times are of academic interest more than anything else, and generally occur on firm or hard going. An animal who establishes a new record may well be something out of the ordinary, though some very moderate horses hold records in this country. Many records have been established with a strong following wind and for this reason would have been declared void on the athletics track. Great store is set by record times in the United States but their races are invariably run flat out from pillar to post.

A further point also of more or less academic interest on which time can throw light is in the comparison of generations. Year after year, for example, people seize upon the time taken to run the Derby as a way of measuring the current classic crop against preceding generations.

Time can be of most practical value in helping to assess the approximate relative ability of two-year-olds during the spring and early summer, when there are few form lines. Comparison is made all the more possible by these races being confined to five and six furlongs, and the fact that minimum distances generally ensure a fast pace throughout.

It is no use making a direct comparison of times, as an easy five furlongs like Epsom's can be run about seven seconds faster than a stiff one like Ascot's. Once again, the best method is to compare the actual time with the Standard for the course in question.

For example, Pip wins a five furlong race at Epsom in 56.2 seconds, which is four fifths of a second above Standard, while Squeak wins a five-furlong race at Lingfield in 57.5 seconds, which is only one-fifth above Standard. On this basis, Squeak is relatively three-fifths of second faster over five furlongs than Pip. The generally accepted formula at this distance is that one-fifteenth of a second equals a pound, so

Squeak appears to be 9 lb. superior to Pip.

Other runners can be brought into the reckoning. Suppose a third horse, Wilfred, had been beaten three lengths by Squeak at Lingfield, he would be considered 9 lb. inferior on the basis of 3 lb. making a difference of one length. In other words, Wilfred can be regarded as being on a par with Pip.

It can be well worth while to build up a comprehensive table of merit, rating at 100 any horse achieving a Standard for the course. One point is added for each winner one-fifth of a second below Standard time, and one point subtracted for each winner one-fifth of a second above Standard. Each performance should be adjusted to what the time would have been had the horse been carrying 9 st. For example, a winner over five furlongs in Standard Time, carrying only 8 st. 5 lb., could have been expected to have taken three-fifths of a second longer had he been carrying 9 st. So his rating would be 97.

A possible snag here is that a better set of Standard Times is likely to be established on a course like Ascot than on a course like Folkestone because of the higher class of racing.

Obviously, two-year-olds will tend to accomplish faster times in the autumn than in the spring when they are less mature. Some courses publish on their racecards the average time of each specific two-year-old race. A youngster who runs considerably faster than the average for his race in the spring is likely to be distinctly useful, even if his time is well above standard.

It is unfortunate that precise calculations about Time can be seriously upset by dissimilar conditions. For instance, had Pip won on good going and in the teeth of half a gale and Squeak won on firm going with a following wind, there would be small wonder that Pip's time compared unfavourably with Squeak's. No one has been able to devise a completely reliable method of measuring the effects of varying conditions on time, although it has been said that heavy going can slow a race down to the tune of a second per furlong. In any case, descriptions on wind and going, however painstakingly reported are usually only inexact expressions of opinion.

The Speed Figures for the first six published under each race in *Raceform*, throw up a steady stream of good priced winners. As their name suggests they are calculated from the race time and a skilfully gauged allowance has been made for the state of the going. The Speed Figures are in fact ratings based entirely on time. Weight adjusted speed figures are published in *Raceform Update* alongside all qualifying entries over a period of a full week.

To sum up, it is wise to back a horse purely on what he has achieved against the clock only when there is a substantial margin in his favour. Some very shrewd operators have made excellent profits by following two-year-old winners who have clocked exceptional times. Conversely, they will not accept highly rated two-year-olds as being top class until they have clocked a fast time. In my opinion, Time is best used as a guide when its findings can be supported by other evidence.

7. *The Draw*

On some courses the draw for places at the start has a devastating influence on the result of the race. It is widely realised, for example, that it is a very considerable disadvantage to be drawn high and on the outside of Chester's round, little course.

The effect of the Draw, which is included among the Racecourse Descriptions at the front of *Raceform Note-Book*, is sometimes aggravated by a prejudice developing among jockeys. If they find they are apparently hopelessly drawn, they may not try quite so hard to win, believing that their chance is negligible. From time to time an enterprising rider will pop up and win on the unfavourable side of the course, rather than tracking over to the "favoured" side and thus explode the effect of the draw as being a myth.

Generally, on a broad straight course, a large field will split into two groups and the race will become virtually two separate races. Even though the draw may have no apparent effect, it is desirable to be on the same side as the faster horses likely to provide the main opposition. It is often worth following a horse who has finished close up while racing alone on the opposite side of the course to his principal rivals. Such a situation can be quickly spotted by using *Raceform Note-Book*. For example, the first six may all be seen to have been drawn high with the exception of the third, who was drawn low.

On some courses the effect of the draw can be influenced by the state of the going. One side may benefit from firm conditions while the other side of the course may have the advantage when the ground is soft. To be certain of the exact state of affairs it is generally necessary to observe the running of earlier races at the meeting. Another factor which can unexpectedly upset the effect of the draw is uneven watering, which is sometimes caused by the wind changing.

The positioning of the stalls on a wide straight course can have a further obvious effect on the draw. Stall positions are announced in the daily racing press.

At certain courses, where one side is favoured and the stalls are placed on that side, some backers have done well with mixed dual forecasts on the four or even six runners drawn on the favoured side. If all goes well, this block of horses will run together and finish together while well fancied horses on the other side are left trailing.

When the going is soft, the ground in the straight on the running side of the round course is liable to get cut up. This results in slowing up the wing of the field drawn on that side in straight races.

8. *Going*

An ability to act on soft or firm going may be inherited. Yet it is noticeable that animals, who win on the soft often succeed also on the hard. Maybe this simply means that they have strong legs and are capable of coping with either extreme of going.

Without doubt the state of the going can provide trainers with an excellent excuse for failure. After an important race it is commonplace for the trainer of some well fancied animal who has finished in the ruck to announce that his charge was seriously inconvenienced by the going, otherwise he surely would have won. And how often do we find that the horse who could not run because apparently it was too firm, is later said to be unable to race because it is too soft?

The moral of this is that we should not be too ready to excuse failure on the score of underfoot conditions. In the majority of instances it is probably wiser to accept the form as it stands.

Nonetheless, a horse who has proved he is capable of winning on a particular type of going will be more likely to win again on similar going. And, incidentally, horses tend to strike winning form at the same time year after year. This interesting fact is catered for by the *Index to Winners* published each year in the front of *Raceform Note-Book*. Here is listed every winner still in training with full details of the months, the courses, the state of the going and the distances at which each has won.

Assessed entirely objectively by Raceform's race-readers, the following range of going descriptions is used in the *Note-Book*: Heavy, soft, yielding, good, fast, firm, hard. The *Note-Book* can vary from the official description issued by the Clerk of the Course or the aforementioned going allowance based on time.

On some courses the going will alter with remarkable rapidity under the influence of rain. One Royal Meeting at Ascot started with firm going but the ground had deteriorated to heavy by the fourth day. When this happens, backers must beware. Newmarket probably boasts the best ground in the country and seldom suffers from extremes.

9. *The Course*

ALTHOUGH some horses seem to keep winning on the same racecourse, there is generally no reason why any horse should prefer one track to another. If, however, a horse does show a special preference it is well worth bearing the point in mind. There may, for example, be evidence that a horse runs better on a left-hand track than on a right-hand track.

A small horse will negotiate turns and gradients better than a large one. A large horse, though, will come into his own on a straight, flat, galloping track.

Previous performances may show that a certain horse sprawls and flounders when he has to gallop downhill. This will clearly be a point against him if he races at such undulating tracks as Epsom, Lingfield or Brighton.

Wide expansive courses with long relentless straights, like Newmarket, call for courage and the ability to maintain a dour gallop.

Conversely, courses with plenty of turns and a short straight are often suitable for horses of dubious character. Such courses make it possible to kid some old rogue past the post and into the winner's enclosure before he even knows he is at the races.

A course which is all on the turn and has virtually no straight is Chester. Its flat, circular track is only just over a mile in circumference and a good deal of luck is required in running. As a result, form at this popular and attractive course tends not to be confirmed elsewhere and form on other courses is not always reproduced at Chester.

Some jockeys shine on particular courses, apparently having their turns and gradients summed up to a T. Piggott at Ascot was a well known example. Ascot with its short straight is not an easy course to ride and apprentices have a poor record there.

Epsom with its tricky downhill run round Tattenham corner is a course which clearly frightens some jockeys, and it is not a course on which to back a two-year-old first time out.

* * *

We have now discussed nine factors, which may throw light on the future running of a racehorse. It should be emphasised that to reach a satisfactory conclusion about the prospects of any runner the backer must be able to consider each of these form factors for himself. Once he has weighed up all the evidence he should be able to reach a verdict.

II. WEIGHT

1. *Collateral Form*

THE case of Alpha and Beta, and their races at Epsom and York, is an example of direct form. Such easy comparisons, where two horses have recently run against each other, are the exception rather than the rule. Generally it is necessary to rely on indirect or collateral form.

For example there may be a third horse called Gamma running in the York race, who has never previously competed against either Alpha or Beta. However, on looking up Gamma's form we find that he finished fourth in a ten furlong handicap at Sandown in July, and that a horse called Delta, who had run sixth to Alpha and Beta at Epsom, finished fifth. The bare bones of the two results appear as follows:

Epsom 10*f. Condition Race for three-year-olds.*			*Sandown* 10*f. Handicap for three-year-olds.*		
Alpha	9—0	... ... —1			
Beta	9—0	... ... 3.2			
		... ... ¾.3			
		... ... ¾.4	Gamma	8—3	 4
		... ... ½.5	Delta	8—12	... ... 1½.5
Delta	9—0	... ... 2.6			

From the Epsom result we see that Delta was four lengths or 8 lb. inferior to Beta. At Sandown Delta, giving 9 lb., was beaten one and a half lengths by Gamma. Gamma therefore, appears to be 6 lb. inferior to Delta, which makes him 14 lb. inferior to Beta.

At York, Beta is set to give Delta only 7 lb. which "strictly on the book" leaves Beta with 7 lb. in hand of Delta.

Frequently an indirect line of form will involve more than one intermediate horse. The more intermediaries there are, the less reliable is the ultimate comparison between two horses likely to be.

It is not unusual for there to be several separate lines of indirect form between two horses. The student hopes that they will all provide the same answer as to their relative merits. But horses are not machines and they do not always reproduce their form exactly. Indeed it is a happy day for the backer if all form lines agree. The question he generally has to face is which line should be accepted and which discarded. Alternatively, should he take a mean between the two? There are some animals who run true to form in almost all their races and thus provide magnificent yardsticks.

Form students generally take the first six places and the distances between them as recorded in *Raceform* and *Raceform Note-Book*. The closer the horses finish to one another, the more accurate the form is likely to be. It stands to reason that if the sixth horse finishes some twenty lengths behind the winner, he is probably being eased by the time he reaches the line. Consequently the result does not reveal his true merit in the same way that it would if he finished sixth in a desperate head and neck affair.

As a very general rule, handicaps, with their larger fields and lightweights setting a good pace, are a more reliable guide to form than weight for ages races.

2. *Weight for Age*

OVERLEAF is the Scale of Weight for Age for flat racing, a vital appendage to the form book whenever horses of different ages run against each other.

The table, which was originally drawn up by Admiral Rous in the latter half of the last century, is not as fearsome as it looks. It simply expresses in exact terms of weight the assumption that horses are almost fully mature and are near the peak of their ability by their fourth year. It shows the rate at which two-year-olds and three-year-olds are likely to improve month by month, although of course there is no guarantee that this improvement will actually take place.

According to the Scale, the Derby winner of the current year would receive 1 st. 1 lb. in late June from the Derby winner of the previous year over a mile and a half.

By early October over the same distance, the difference would be only 8 lb., as the younger animal would be expected to have shown relative improvement.

The weight concession to four-year-olds by their elders is nil in these days of early maturity. Furthermore, two-year-olds seldom take on older horses so all the form student need really trouble about is the relative improvement to be expected month by month in a three-year-old. In passing, it is worth noting that the Weight for Age Scale definitely seems to favour two-year-olds when they do take on their

SCALE OF WEIGHT FOR AGE

Expressed as the number of pounds that is deemed the average horse in each group falls short of maturity at different dates and distances.

Distance Furlongs	Age	JAN 1/15	JAN 16/31	FEB 1/14	FEB 15/28	MARCH 1/15	MARCH 16/31	APRIL 1/15	APRIL 16/30	MAY 1/15	MAY 16/31	JUNE 1/15	JUNE 16/30	JULY 1/15	JULY 16/31	AUGUST 1/15	AUGUST 16/31	SEPT 1/15	SEPT 16/30	OCT 1/15	OCT 16/31	NOV 1/15	NOV 16/30	DEC 1/15	DEC 16/31
5	2	—	—	—	—	—	47	44	41	38	36	34	32	30	28	26	24	22	20	19	18	17	17	16	16
	3	15	15	15	15	14	13	12	11	10	9	8	7	6	5	4	3	2	2	1	1	—	—	—	—
6	2	—	—	—	—	—	—	—	—	44	41	38	36	33	31	28	26	24	22	21	20	19	18	17	17
	3	16	16	16	16	15	14	13	12	11	10	9	8	7	6	5	4	3	3	2	2	1	1	—	—
7	2	—	—	—	—	—	—	—	—	—	—	—	—	38	35	32	30	27	25	23	22	21	20	19	19
	3	18	18	18	18	17	16	15	14	12	11	10	9	8	7	6	5	4	4	3	3	2	2	1	1
8	2	—	—	—	—	—	—	—	—	—	—	—	—	—	—	37	34	31	28	26	24	23	22	21	20
	3	20	20	19	19	18	17	16	15	13	12	11	10	9	8	7	6	5	4	4	3	3	2	2	1
	4	1	1	—	—	—	—	—	—	—	—	—	—	—	—	—	—	—	—	—	—	—	—	—	—
9	3	22	22	21	20	20	19	18	17	15	14	12	11	10	9	8	7	6	5	5	4	4	3	2	2
	4	2	2	1	1	1	—	—	—	—	—	—	—	—	—	—	—	—	—	—	—	—	—	—	—
10	3	23	23	22	22	21	20	19	18	16	15	13	12	11	10	9	8	7	6	6	5	5	4	4	3
	4	3	3	2	2	1	1	—	—	—	—	—	—	—	—	—	—	—	—	—	—	—	—	—	—
11	3	—	—	—	—	23	22	21	20	18	17	15	14	12	11	10	9	8	7	7	6	6	5	4	4
	4	4	4	3	3	2	1	1	—	—	—	—	—	—	—	—	—	—	—	—	—	—	—	—	—
12	3	—	—	—	—	24	23	22	21	19	18	16	15	13	12	11	10	9	8	8	7	7	6	6	5
	4	5	4	4	3	3	2	2	1	—	—	—	—	—	—	—	—	—	—	—	—	—	—	—	—
13	3	—	—	—	—	25	24	23	22	20	19	17	16	14	13	12	11	10	9	8	8	7	6	6	5
	4	5	4	4	3	3	2	2	1	—	—	—	—	—	—	—	—	—	—	—	—	—	—	—	—
14	3	—	—	—	—	26	25	24	23	21	20	18	17	15	14	13	12	11	10	9	9	8	7	7	6
	4	6	5	5	4	4	3	3	2	1	—	—	—	—	—	—	—	—	—	—	—	—	—	—	—
15	3	—	—	—	—	28	27	26	25	23	21	19	18	16	15	14	13	12	11	10	9	9	8	7	6
	4	6	5	5	4	4	3	3	2	2	1	—	—	—	—	—	—	—	—	—	—	—	—	—	—
16	3	—	—	—	—	29	28	27	26	24	22	20	19	17	16	15	14	13	12	11	10	10	9	8	7
	4	7	7	6	6	5	5	4	4	3	2	1	—	—	—	—	—	—	—	—	—	—	—	—	—
18	3	—	—	—	—	31	30	29	28	26	24	22	21	19	18	17	16	15	14	13	12	11	10	9	8
	4	8	8	7	7	6	6	5	5	4	3	2	1	—	—	—	—	—	—	—	—	—	—	—	—
20	3	—	—	—	—	33	32	31	30	28	26	24	22	20	19	18	17	16	15	14	13	12	11	10	9
	4	9	9	8	8	7	7	6	6	5	4	3	2	1	—	—	—	—	—	—	—	—	—	—	—

seniors. The former Nunthorpe Stakes at York, one of the acknowledged sprint championship events, often used to see a second grade youngster finishing close up to top older sprinters.

Application of the table is easy, as the following example will show. A three-year-old, carrying 8 st. 4 lb., in a five furlong handicap at the beginning of June. The four-year-old beats the three-year-old by two lengths, which is equivalent to 6 lb. It appears therefore, that the four-year-old is the three-year-old's superior by 18 lb. at that time.

The two meet again in another five furlong handicap at the end of October. This time, the four-year-old is set to carry 9 st. 1 lb. and the three-year-old 8 st. 2 lb. From the table we find that the three-year-old should have improved by 9 lb. during the intervening five months. This is ascertained by taking the difference at five furlongs between the early June and the late October columns. We would therefore expect the three-year-old to receive 10 lb. on the strength of his performance in June. However, he is receiving 13 lb., which on the face of it gives him 3 lb. the better of it with the four-year-old.

Where apprentice riders are concerned, it is clearly wise to add any weight allowance to the actual weight carried before making calculations. However, it may be preferable not to do this in the case of exceptionally talented apprentices, deemed to be worth more than their allowance.

3. *Assessing Chances*

By a series of direct and indirect form calculations it is possible to make an assessment of the relative chances of most runners in a race. Each assessment should be based on the horse's best performance, which after all is what he should be capable of reproducing once again. Whether or not he will in fact run to his best form is another matter and it is up to the backer to judge the likelihood of his doing so before he strikes a bet.

Naturally, if a horse has failed to produce his best form for some considerable time, it is reasonable to suppose that he has deteriorated and that he is no longer capable of achieving that form. In the circumstances it will be wise to rate the horse on a more lowly mark, based on his best recent performance. The period of time which should be allowed to elapse before a horse is relegated in this way depends on how frequently he has been seriously fancied to win.

There may be every justification for down-grading a horse after three or four races within a period of a couple of months. It would not be wise to do this however, if it were considered that there were other factors such as going, draw or jockeyship, which had been stopping the animal from running up to his best.

Sometimes a horse will not show his true form for as long as two years, but he may only have been stopped from doing so through some set-back in training or through conditions always being against him. Indeed, as a rule, it is safer not to write down a horse too quickly.

As a very rough guide, a two-year-old (or any older horse for that matter) can be expected to show 7 lb. improvement as a result of his first race. Thus, if a two-year-old with experience beats another having his first race by a length, the result is quite likely to be reversed when they meet again on the same terms.

When making his mathematical assessment the handicapper, whether he be of the official or the private variety, must decide to what extent, if at all, he is going to alter his figures on account of incidents in the running of a previous race. If he sees that a horse has won comfortably, should he raise his rating of the winner on this score? If so, by how many pounds?

Likewise, if a horse started slowly in a sprint race, should he upgrade him in relation to the bare result?

Such conundrums can only be tackled on their merits and are best left to the judgment of the individual concerned.

4. *Handicaps*

WHEN assessing in terms of weight the chance of all the horses in a race based on their previous form, you are in fact framing a handicap. Compare this private handicap with the actual weights to be carried in the race and it will reveal which horses have the best chance at the weights. For example, you may calculate that Faith should have 9 st. 3 lb., Hope 9 st., and Charity 8 st. 10 lb. If in fact, they are all set to carry 9 st., Hope, in your opinion, will have the correct weight, while Faith has 3 lb. too little and Charity 4 lb. too much. For convenience, the assessment is expressed as follows:

Faith	–3
Hope	—
Charity	+4

In a weight-for-age race, you may possibly find that the horse with the best chance appears to have as much as 2 st. in hand of the horse with the least chance. On the other hand, in a handicap the range is likely to be very much less, possibly no more than 7 lb. or so. After all, you and the official handicapper are working on the same form figures and your conclusions should not be greatly at variance. The most likely reason for your assessment of any horse to vary substantially from that of the official is if it has shown a variation in form after the handicap was published.

The conditions of any handicap decree what range of weights may be used on the day. The original handicap may have allowed some of the runners considerably less than this bottom weight. According to the official handicapper their chance is negligible. Your figures may or may not confirm this view.

At the height of his career the mighty Arkle was about 2 st. superior to almost every other steeplechaser in training. When he ran in a handicap practically all his competitors thus had to be bulked together with bottom weight, which meant that "on the book" most of them had no chance.

Penalties are another factor which will throw the official handicap. A winner since the publication of weights has to carry a purely arbitrary extra poundage, which may vary according to the value of the race or races won or the amount of weight he was originally set to carry. Some years ago the conditions of a sponsored handicap allowed the handicapper to re-assess each winner according to the merit of his victory, but this experiment has not become general practice.

Having completed an assessment of a race, it is unlikely that you will wish to follow its findings blindly, unless perhaps one horse is shown to have several pounds in hand of any other. Your wisest course of action may be to take, say, the four horses best in at the weights and examine their credentials more thoroughly. The various factors which already have been discussed will come into consideration. If you are at the races, paddock condition and the betting exchanges may influence your final choice. Otherwise you may be swayed by the jockey, the going, the course, the distance, the draw and, very particularly, whether or not the horse in question seems to be running into form or losing form.

It has been estimated that few handicappers deal with

more than a dozen horses an hour, if rating their chances from scratch, which gives some idea of the time required. The average racing enthusiast with a mass of workaday commitments will be unable to spare the time to compile a handicap assessment for more than a few races.

A better way is to maintain a universal handicap of as many horses as possible and extract the weights for a particular race either at entry or overnight.

A method of keeping the framework of a handicap is to work out a rating for each winner and enter the figures race-by-race in the form book. From this skeleton it is possible to arrive at an assessment for other horses who finished in the first six. Even so a great deal of compilation is involved before arriving at a complete assessment for any race and, in most cases, it will be necessary to work back through several races before a satisfactory rating can be decided upon for any horse. Because of limited time, many amateur handicappers concentrate on certain categories of races, such as sprint handicaps or two-year-old events.

Many professional racing men prefer to rely on the assessments provided by *Raceform Private Handicap*, which is compiled by experts and has been published regularly for almost 60 years. The entries for each race are listed in order of their chances at the weights, the one with the best chance appearing at the head of the list.

Raceform Private Handicap's master ratings appear in the index of *Raceform Note-Book*. These represent the best mark at which the private handicappers have assessed each individual and which they believe it still capable of attaining. A performance rating for each race appears after each note and this reveals whether a horse has run up to its master rating and whether it is on the upgrade or downgrade compared with recent performances.

III. INFORMATION

WHEREAS Form covers matters of common knowledge and of opinion on public performance, Information covers news of a private nature which normally would be known only to the immediate connections of a racehorse.

A horse's general well-being and state of fitness come under the heading of Information, as do the results of private gallops on the training grounds.

Obviously the trainer is better placed than anyone else to obtain such knowledge. But one or two intimate items of this sort may be gleaned at first hand by stable employees and jockeys closely connected with the stable, or at second hand from the trainer. Most stable lads' gossip, though, is notoriously misleading and jockeys have a reputation for being poor tipsters.

In addition to what goes on at home, an experienced jockey may have invaluable knowledge about a horse's running on the racecourse, which could only be gained at first hand by a participant in the race.

Unless he rides work, the owner does not usually have the means to acquire first hand information for himself. He has to rely on what he is told by the trainer, and possibly by the jockey. A few owners, however, are excellent judges of form and play an expert part in the placing of their horses, but the bases for their calculations are generally also available to any member of the general public.

On the other hand, some trainers and owners are poor judges of form and are less good at assessing their charges' chances than are many ordinary racing enthusiasts. Excellent stableman though he may be, it is no use a trainer bringing a horse to peak fitness with a view to winning a particular race if he has hopelessly underestimated the opposition.

Many trainers, particularly those with vast strings, simply do not have time under present day conditions and the massive fixture list to make a profound study of form. They will know that their horse is fit and well, and has done all that has been asked of him at home. They will run him in a convenient race and hope for the best. In the circumstances, they will not be tempted to have a particularly large bet, but will make no secret of the fact that the horse is mildly fancied.

Anyone who hears directly or indirectly from owner or trainer that the horse is fit and fancied obviously has some useful information though it will not be sufficient to unduly influence his calculations. Owners and trainers who forecast that their horse has an each way chance are usually, in the experience of the author, displaying a certain lack of confidence. The runner in question invariably finishes fourth!

Some stables, of course, are well known for their skill at placing their horses to win. These are mostly stables which like to have a good bet from time to time on a carefully planned near-certainty. In such cases, the essence of the operation is secrecy and no information will be allowed to leak out until the stable money is on at the best possible prices.

Inspired bets of this sort will be reflected by the betting market. In fact, the bookmakers automatically become the repository of any information from those stables which like to have a bet. Whereas £50 may represent a confident bet for one stable, £500 may be needed to indicate confidence by another. Whether the bets are placed direct or through an agent, the bookmakers have a knack of gauging the degree of confidence behind inspired money. The recipient of the original bet may decide to back the horse for himself and so good money soon starts to snowball and the price comes tumbling down.

Previously it was only possible to observe the market fluctuations on the racecourse itself or on a tape machine. Nowadays the ordinary punter has more opportunities, either through television or through the local betting shops.

The more the racegoer attends meetings, the more people he will get to know and the more tips he will be given. The same applies to the off-course racing enthusiast who associates with others of similar inclination.

Most of this so called "information" will be tenth or eleventh hand, highly exaggerated, unreliable and generally useless. In other words, most of it can be safely ignored. But just occasionally a particular informant will prove to have reliable sources of information and will be worth listening to. He should be cultivated and, as one good turn deserves another, should be told in exchange anything interesting the backer may know and feels he can pass on.

In addition there are the professional tipsters who offer to sell information about which they make extravagant claims.

Before purchasing their wares, just ask yourself the question: Why, if this information is really so good, does not the tipster make his fortune betting on his own account without bothering to sell the news to others?

Some tipsters may have genuine sources of information or they may just be good judges of the form book. But, on the whole, the average newspaper racing correspondent who is at the races every day and knows a host of useful people, will be infinitely better informed and will be a better judge.

To conclude this chapter, it should be stressed that good information is by no means easy to come by and, in the case of the majority of races there is probably no inside information about any of the runners which could be of any real value. The more information circulates, the less reliable and the more exaggerated it tends to become. A friendly bookmaker can often prove the best source of news. Before following even the most reliable information with hard cash, it is desirable to obtain some sort of confirmation through the form book. In most cases, the form book is likely to prove by far the more reliable guide.

IV. METHODICAL BETTING

1. *The Businesslike Approach*

So far we have discussed ways and means of finding winners. Given reasonable success in this sphere, it is also vitally important that the backer should conduct his betting operations to the best possible advantage.

Most people back horses "just for fun". Splendid entertainment though it is, betting cannot be approached in this frame of mind if it is to be made to pay. It must be tackled in a businesslike manner and treated like any other serious enterprise in which money is involved. Goodness knows, it has never been easy to show a regular profit backing horses. Professional backers expect nothing much more than 2½ per cent profit on their annual turnover. With a 10% deduction, the off-course punter really has got the odds stacked against him.

It is essential to bet methodically. For a start, this means keeping a precise record which will reveal at once the state of profit or loss. Surprisingly few punters take the trouble to do this and as a result many are under the illusion that they are winning when in fact they may be showing a sizeable loss.

It is desirable to set aside a definite sum of money as a betting bank. If this is expended, a halt should be called to betting operations, for the time being. Some people find it convenient to open a separate account at their bank for this purpose, which gives them the added advantage of having their book-keeping done for them.

A sensible way of proceeding is to stake a fraction of the bank for each bet, say a fiftieth or a twenty-fifth. For convenience, this fraction need not be varied after every bet, but rather at the end of each week or other convenient period. This method has the advantage of reducing stakes on a bad run and increasing them on a good one.

Greed has been the undoing of many a backer. Rather than go to the races with five pounds and the aim of winning fifty, it is more businesslike to take fifty pounds and aim to win five. By so doing, the chances of profit in the long term are infinitely increased.

Although a systematic approach to betting is strongly urged, betting systems are not advocated. Even if a system which will show a profit year after year exists, it seems extremely doubtful whether its inventor would wish to divulge its details.

Neither are staking plans recommended. Any method of finding winners which cannot produce a profit to a level stake is not worth troubling about. Winning or losing sequences cannot be predicted, and it is just sheer luck if one staking plan happens to show a greater profit than another. Backers who are unable to resist staking plans are strongly advised to adopt one which involves increasing bets after winners rather than increasing bets after losers. Doubling up in order to recoup losses can be the quickest route to the workhouse.

The only other sensible alternative to level stake betting is a variable stake which gives the backer the same size win whatever the odds. In other words, if he places £10 on an even-money chance, he would stake only £1 on a 10/1 chance. With most bookmakers deducting tax from the stake and winnings of winning bets only, the nett profit is greater on the longer priced bets. For the average backer, it is in any case difficult to gauge his variable stake precisely as he can only guess at the likely starting price. Some credit bookmakers, though, will accept instructions that the client wishes to bet on a horse to win a specific sum.

Talking of tax, the off-course backer has the option of paying the tax on his stake rather than paying nothing on losing bets and having a deduction from both winnings and stakes on all winning bets. As most backers are net losers in the long run, it is more realistic not to pay tax when placing the bet. However, we must be optimistic so maybe its best to pay the tax at the outset particularly if we are especially confident.

The backer's one great advantage over the bookmaker is that he can choose when to bet. As far as possible, every race should be regarded as a prospective betting medium but the backer should strike only when he considers that he is getting good value for money.

Bookmakers stand to win more over doubles, trebles and especially accumulators. If you must go in for multiple bets, at least avoid any special series of races selected by the bookmakers, they are bound to be the most difficult to solve! Even though there may be a consolation prize for a near-miss, it is much better to pick out for yourself the races on which you wish to wager.

Patience is essential and never let it be forgotten that to miss backing a loser is as good as backing an even money winner. Though obviously it is more fun always to have an interest, the racegoer or television viewer is not giving himself a chance if he insists on having a bet on every race. He should not allow himself even to have a small nominal bet in those races for which he has no strong fancy. Small losses can soon add up and dissipate winnings from the more inspired bets. Restraint must also be shown in betting on the glamour races like the Lincoln, the Hunt Cup and the Cambridgeshire. These popular events very often do not present satisfactory betting opportunities and can best be described as bookmakers' benefits. Likewise, many backers choose to go to war at the big festival meetings like Epsom, Royal Ascot, Goodwood, York, Doncaster and Cheltenham. Generally speaking, they will find winner-finding easier at the run of the mill meetings and on the whole they should avoid handicaps.

2. *The Best Time to Bet*

So far as four-year-olds and older horses are concerned, the previous season's form can be of very real value in the spring. But this is not so with the three-year-olds.

Season after season, many of the top two-year-olds of the previous year fail to make normal improvement during the winter and juvenile form is turned upside down when they re-appear as three-year-olds. Fillies, in particular, are notorious for their failure to train on in their second season, especially those who were heavily raced as youngsters. Henry Cecil, for instance, does not believe in racing any potentially useful three-year-old more than three times during its two-year-old season unless he thinks the owner is unlikely to survive the winter!

It is therefore inadvisable to take a short price about a three-year-old making his seasonal debut. Let him show his paces on the racecourse first, and then perhaps back him next time.

Although form is naturally scanty, the opening weeks of the flat racing season can be most lucrative for the backer who is in a position to follow the market. At this time of year, competition is apt to be less severe and only a limited number of runners may be fancied. The market will soon reveal which these are. During April, it is well worth following horses which have already had a race and run well.

Throughout the year, two-year-olds run truer to form than the older age groups and early two-year-old races can provide good opportunities for investment. A smart winning juvenile is often worth following until beaten. Moreover his price will sometimes be comparatively generous if and when he meets unraced animals with big home reputations. Such youngsters are apt to run green, and in any case their connections will probably not wish them to be given an unduly hard race first time out. In addition to these two considerations, it is always a better proposition to take the horse with the public form rather than the horse with the private form.

Late April and May often produce a period of form upsets. Fitness is no longer at a premium and horses, who failed to show their form in the early spring, start turning the tables on their successful rivals.

Possibly the factor which upsets form more radically than any other is a violent change in the going, which, of course, is brought about by a sudden change in weather conditions.

Conversely, a long dry summer with consistently fast going can provide the backer with a rich harvest. Admittedly the fields may be small, especially at the lesser meetings. But profits are likely to be steadier when competition is reduced, even though they may be less spectacular.

Some of the shrewdest backers confine their betting to the period mid-June to mid-September, as this is the time when form is at its most reliable. A three-year-old filly who hits form in late summer is often worth following for the next month or two, as she may continue to show spectacular physical improvement under the warm sun. Also, it is in July that the three-year-olds start to beat their elders. In nursery handicaps, a popular system is to back runners who have had one winning race only. The theory is that the handicapper may not have managed to assess their full merit on such sparse evidence and they may be a great deal better than he thinks. In the old days, no entry could be made for a nursery until the two-year-old concerned had run three times.

The autumn rains, horses losing their form and the scramble to earn the winter's keep make winner finding increasingly difficult during the back-end. Few backers would find themselves losers if they firmly resolved to close their betting book during the early days of October.

Certainly there is little to be gained in attempting to continue until the turf season reaches its bitter end.

Throughout the year, any horse which has been supplemented for a major race is well worth the closest inspection. A very high entry fee has been paid at the eleventh hour and obviously connections would have done this only if they fancied their chances more than a little.

Though racing over fences and hurdles has been mentioned only superficially in this book, the weeks immediately following the end of flat racing often prove the most lucrative period of the whole year for the punter. The jumping season has been gradually warming up since August and there is plenty of form in the book. On the other hand, competition is generally not too severe and the pre-Christmas weather generally does not cause serious dislocation through frost and snow.

After Christmas, winner-finding becomes more difficult. Almost every runner is out to win as trainers believe that they must seize their opportunities while the frost and snow keep away. Some meetings inevitably have to be cancelled and the weather interferes with training programmes with a result that some runners are not fit to do themselves justice. After a hold-up, the fittest horses are generally those that were in form before the weather clamped down.

Although often considered as the dullest form of racing, fancied runners in novice hurdles may in the long term provide the best betting medium of all because of the poor quality of much of the opposition. The fact that many bookmakers will not accept each way bets in novice hurdles provides backers with a significant pointer.

All-Weather racing is the subject of a separate book, "Win at All-Weather Racing" by Tony Stafford. Suffice it to say here that form on the turf does not always work out on the dirt and vice-versa.

V. OBTAINING VALUE

In the first edition of this book, published in 1962, a chapter was devoted to each way betting. In it was demonstrated that only in a field of eight runners did the backer have the advantage with place bets at a quarter the odds. Most bookmakers now offer only a fifth the odds a place, and consequently each way betting is no longer value for money. It seldom was value in big handicap fields — even in the old days. Many punters liked to bet each way in these open events, but now more than ever they would be better advised to divert their place stake on to a second runner to win.

The clever bet in the old days was to go for the second or third favourite each way in a conditions race with a really warm first favourite and about eight to 12 runners. Often in such races only three or four runners were seriously fancied and the each way bets caught the bookmakers on a vulnerable spot. Backers who concentrated on each way bets of this type often used to find their accounts being closed. The Betting Tax and the old Selective Employment Tax, which bookmakers used as an excuse years ago for altering their each way betting rules, have thus helped "the enemy" to close a chink in their armour.

What applied to each way betting is also true of win only bets. Quite apart from the obvious difficulty of trying to find the winner of a handicap, bookmakers bet to a wider profit margin in these events than they do in the average condition race. Best value is normally to be obtained in condition races with six or seven runners, where only two or three have any real chance.

Obtaining value must be the keystone of successful betting. If you fancy a horse and assess its chances in a race as 50/50, and are then able to back at 2/1 against, you are obviously obtaining excellent value. To make an accurate assessment of a horse's chance is easier said than done and anyone who has such a facility to an unfailing degree would be certain to make money in the long run. Nevertheless, any backer with a fair knowledge of form should be able to recognise the not-uncommon instances when a horse is being offered at unreasonably short odds. Even if he confidently expects the horse to win, he should avoid backing it if the odds do not represent value for money. *Raceform Private Handicap* offers a reliable check in such matters. If an odds-on favourite, for example, is poorly rated, it is most unlikely that it is worth a bet.

Early skirmishers can often obtain value as the offices open in the morning from those bookmakers who advertise prices about some of the day's more important races. Newspaper betting forecasts sometimes can help you to spot if your fancy is likely to start at more contracted odds than those advertised.

Backers with the facilities to do so will often lay a horse which they consider is being offered at a thoroughly false price. As an alternative, the ordinary backer can bet on two or three others to beat a false favourite.

It should not be imagined from the foregoing that a backer should never bet odds-on, but he should be satisfied that the horse in question is entitled to be at considerably longer odds-on. In the old days, some shrewd operators would leave their bookmakers a standing order for everything starting at 2/1 on or shorter on the premise that at such odds they must be unbeatable. Nowadays, the usual practice of deducting ten per cent off-course from both stake and winnings effectively reduces a 2/1 on bet to almost 3/1 on. With a 10/1 on winner, the absurd situation arises whereby the backer is actually out of pocket.

Professional backers are seldom attracted to betting on the Tote pools, as they cannot tell in advance what sort of value they are getting. Nonetheless there are occasions when win or place bets on the Tote generally prove attractive. Outsiders, offered by the bookmakers at 6-1 and above, are likely to pay better on the Tote, as shown in the table opposite. If a big betting stable places a very late commission with the bookmakers and thus contracts the price of one of its runners at the last moment, the Tote again may hold the advantage for the speedy backer. Where a well known horse starts a very warm favourite at a big meeting, it often will pay a remarkably good price for a win or place on the Tote. The general public normally will not consider having a place bet on a raging favourite and so the shrewd backer can cash in with such a bet. For the same sort of reason, a dual forecast on the first two favourites, where appropriate, can be rewarding.

As I have previously remarked, bookmakers welcome accumulator bets as the more horses are involved the greater is the margin of profit. If you are enough of an optimist to attempt an accumulator for goodness sake choose the races which give you the best chance, and not those which are specified for you in bookmakers' advertisements.

COMPARISON OF TOTALISATOR DIVIDENDS WITH S.P. ODDS FLAT SEASON 1991

S.P. WIN ODDS	No. of dividends	Tote better than S.P.	S.P. better than Tote	Tote & S.P. Equal
UNDER 1-2	83	51	28	4
1-2 & OVER	220	89	122	9
EVENS	60	26	27	7
11-10	46	17	20	9
6-5	19	6	9	4
5-4	50	20	30	—
11-8	55	27	28	—
6-4	81	29	42	10
13-8	44	10	34	—
7-4	86	29	57	—
15-8	49	16	33	—
2-1	105	37	57	11
85-40	8	1	7	—
9-4	114	52	62	—
95-40	1	1	0	—
5-2	100	38	54	8
11-4	106	41	65	—
3-1	153	53	88	12
10-3	57	24	33	—
7-2	152	60	84	8
4-1	187	76	107	4
9-2	138	48	85	5
5-1	180	71	104	5
11-2	121	48	66	7
6-1	169	75	91	3
13-2	87	50	36	1
7-1	140	73	65	2
15-2	33	19	14	—
8-1	162	88	71	3
17-2	9	6	3	—
9-1	81	42	39	—
10-1	160	93	67	—
11-1	37	27	10	—
12-1	132	79	51	2
14-1	118	74	44	—
16-1	99	69	30	—
20-1	75	54	21	—
25-1	42	30	12	—
28-1	1	0	1	—
33-1	43	29	14	—
50-1	8	1	7	—
66-1	3	0	3	—
TOTALS	3617	1680	1823	114
Percentage of Total		46.44	50.40	3.15

The Tote Jackpot represents value when a good carry forward has built up as a result of the pool not being won on previous days. When outsiders win, the Jackpot generally pays better than the corresponding starting price accumulator.

A complete book on the subject of obtaining value was published by Raceform a year ago. Written by Malcolm Howard, a qualified accountant, it is entitled "The Value Factor in Successful Betting." Copies are still available by post at £5.95 from Raceform Ltd., Compton, Newbury, Berkshire.

VI. ANTE POST BETTING AND BETTING TO FIGURES

VERY often Ante Post prices are far from generous and offer little advantage over those available on the day of the race.

The bookmakers are compelled to pursue a cautious policy. So often they find that the public are interested in backing only one or two horses and seldom does the betting take a really wide range until close to the day of the race. If public interest is lacking, the only money bookmakers are likely to attract is from inspired stable sources. And they may burn their fingers on that sort of money, finding perhaps by the day of the race that they have laid the favourite and second favourite only and at longer odds than are available on the course.

Before striking an Ante Post bet, the punter should have the knowledge that his fancy is an intended runner. There is always the risk that a mishap in training will stop the horse from running, but it is obviously ridiculous to throw away good money on an animal whose connections are not intending to send him to the post.

By moving fast and early the punter can sometimes get himself a bargain especially on Saturday morning where an enterprising bookmaker has published Ante Post lists on two or three races due to be contested that afternoon. The backer may be able to spot a horse who stands at obviously attractive odds before the other backers have done so.

At any one time a bookmaker will of course arrange his prices to produce a margin of profit provided the whole field is backed proportionately. However, the backer may be able to make use of fluctuations in the market to get the best odds about several runners. In the end, he may be able to ensure himself a profit by covering every runner.

Such an operation, which is known as making a Backer's Book, need not be confined to Ante Post races. In fact there are a few professional backers who make a steady living by betting to figures on the racecourse. There is no reason why the amateur should not indulge in this intriguing pursuit, but success demands astuteness and quick thinking. It is essential to be able to assess whether a price represents good value for money or not.

In most races, the backer will prefer to go for a greater profit by taking a view and leaving several of the runners out of his calculations. He may decide that the race lies between three or four horses and ignore the rest. Here is a very simple example. Imagine a three horse race between A, B and C. Our backer friend considers that C has no chance. A and B are thought to have about the same chance and the betting opens 4/5 A, 5/4 B, 10/1 C. The backer takes £10 to £8 about B. After a while, support for B causes the bookmakers to lay even money each of two and finally to make B favourite at 4/5. A eases to 5/4 and our backer moves to strike a bet of £10 to £8. No matter whether A or B wins, the backer shows a gross profit of £2. Success for the outsider C would of course result in his losing £16.

The majority of races will present a more complicated problem than this and the backer will have to be able to translate odds into chances in order to evaluate his profit margin. This is done simply by adding up both sides of the odds and placing the result under the right hand side of the odds. Thus odds of 4-1 can be expressed as a 1/5th, while odds of 1-4 can be expressed as 4/5ths.

To save adding fractions it is preferable to express them as percentages, through multiplying each fraction by 100. Thus 1/5th is 20 per cent and 4/5ths is 80 per cent. On the next page is a fairly comprehensive table of odds expressed as chances in percentages.

Naturally, on the racecourse it is only practical to bet to the nearest pound or round sum and it is necessary therefore to adjust stakes accordingly.

Supposing a backer considers that the race lies between horses X, Y and Z and decides to back them each to yield £100 including his stake. He manages to get 3/1, 4/1 and 10/1 against their chances respectively. From the table we see that this will involve an outlay of £25 + £20 + £9.10 = £54.10 — and, provided one of the three wins, a profit of £45.90 will be realised.

The better the odds the backer is able to obtain, the greater his profit will be.

The 10% deduction, which plagues the off-course backer, has been laboured rather heavily here. Those who cannot go racing, and thus take advantage of betting tax free, can at least shop around in search of one of the smaller bookmakers who deduct as little as 7% or even 6%.

Odds	Odds agst. Chance	Odds on Chance	Odds	Odds agst. Chance	Odds on Chance
Evens	50.0	50	6/1	14.3	85.7
5/4	44.4	55.6	7/1	12.5	87.5
6/4	40	60	8/1	11.1	88.9
7/4	36.4	63.6	10/1	9.1	90.9
2/1	33.3	66.7	11/1	8.3	91.6
9/4	30.8	69.2	12/1	7.4	92.3
5/2	28.6	71.4	14/1	6.6	93.3
11/4	26.7	73.3	16/1	5.8	94.1
3/1	25	75	20/1	4.8	95.2
7/2	22.2	77.8	25/1	3.8	90.2
4/1	20	80	33/1	3	97
9/2	18.2	81.8	40/1	2.4	97.6
5/1	16.7	83.3	50/1	2	98

In conclusion and at the risk of stressing the obvious, every backer should be constantly trying to reduce his proportion of losing bets. Exercise patience and never forget that to miss a loser is better than backing an 11-10 winner after the deductions at 10%.